PRINTED IN THE UNITED STATES OF AMERICA

978-0-9993441-5-6
FIRST PRINTING, 2020

MARRO PRESS
KATY, TX
MARROPRESS@GMAIL.COM

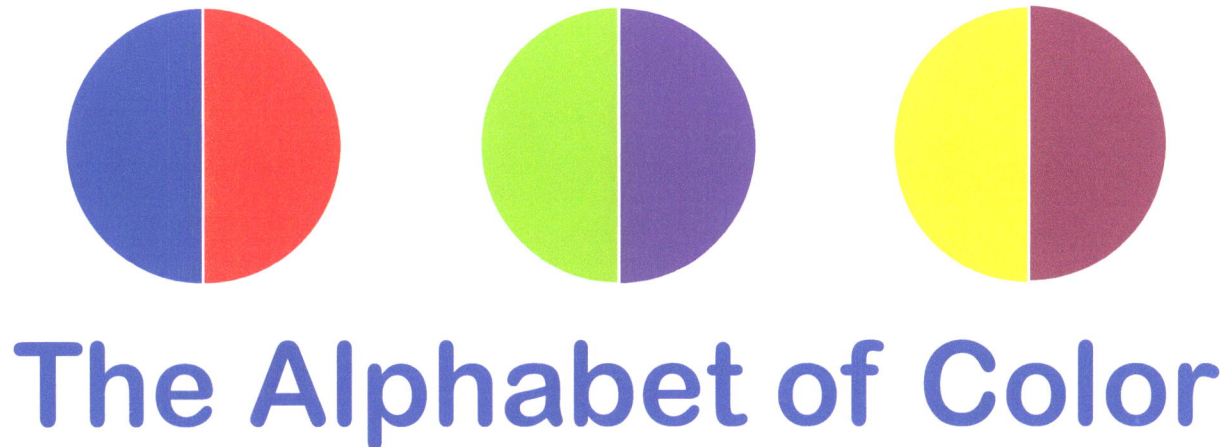

The Alphabet of Color

From Amaranth to Zucchini

Written by Robin Oloyede

This book is dedicated to all the little artists and color lovers.

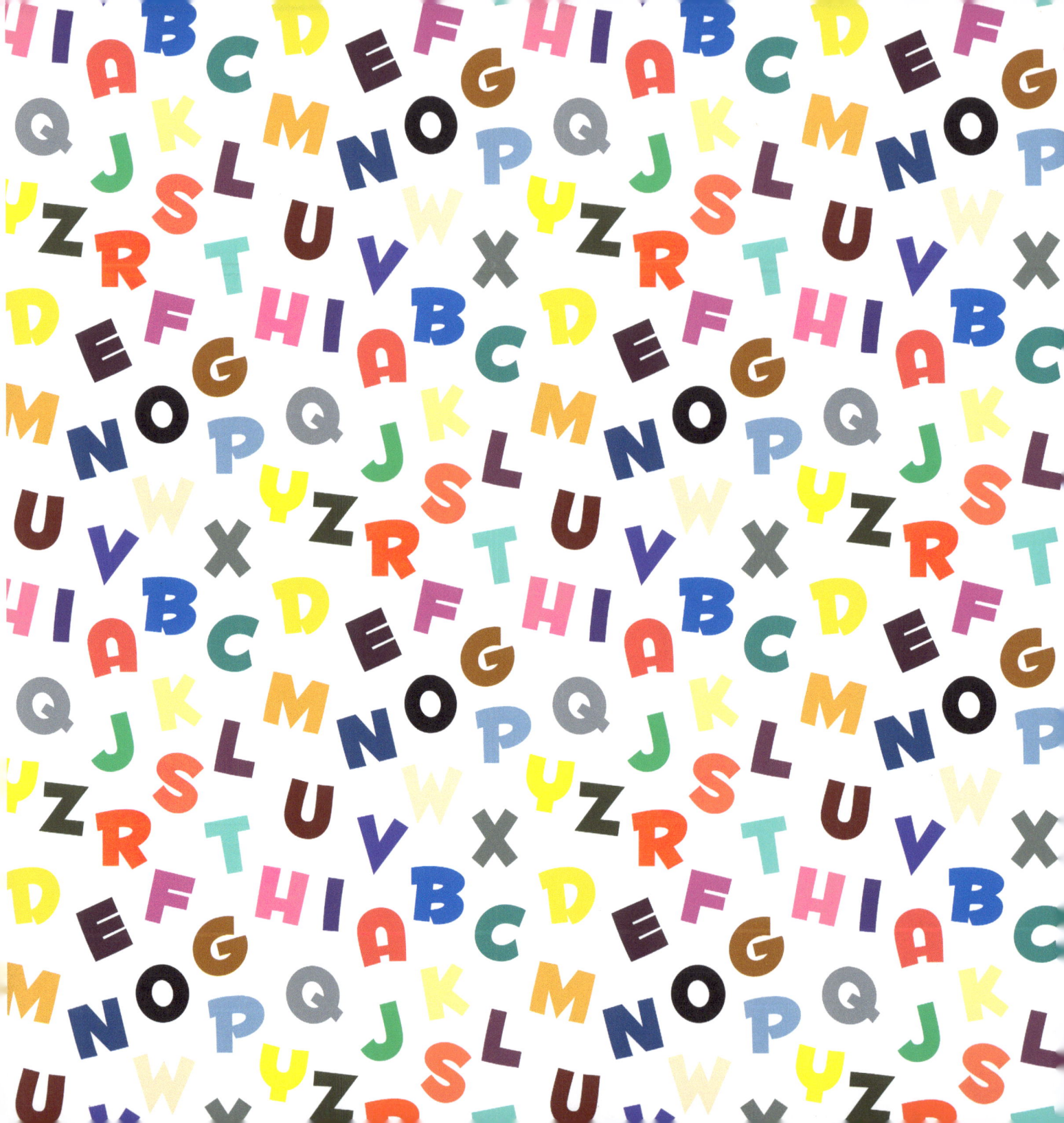

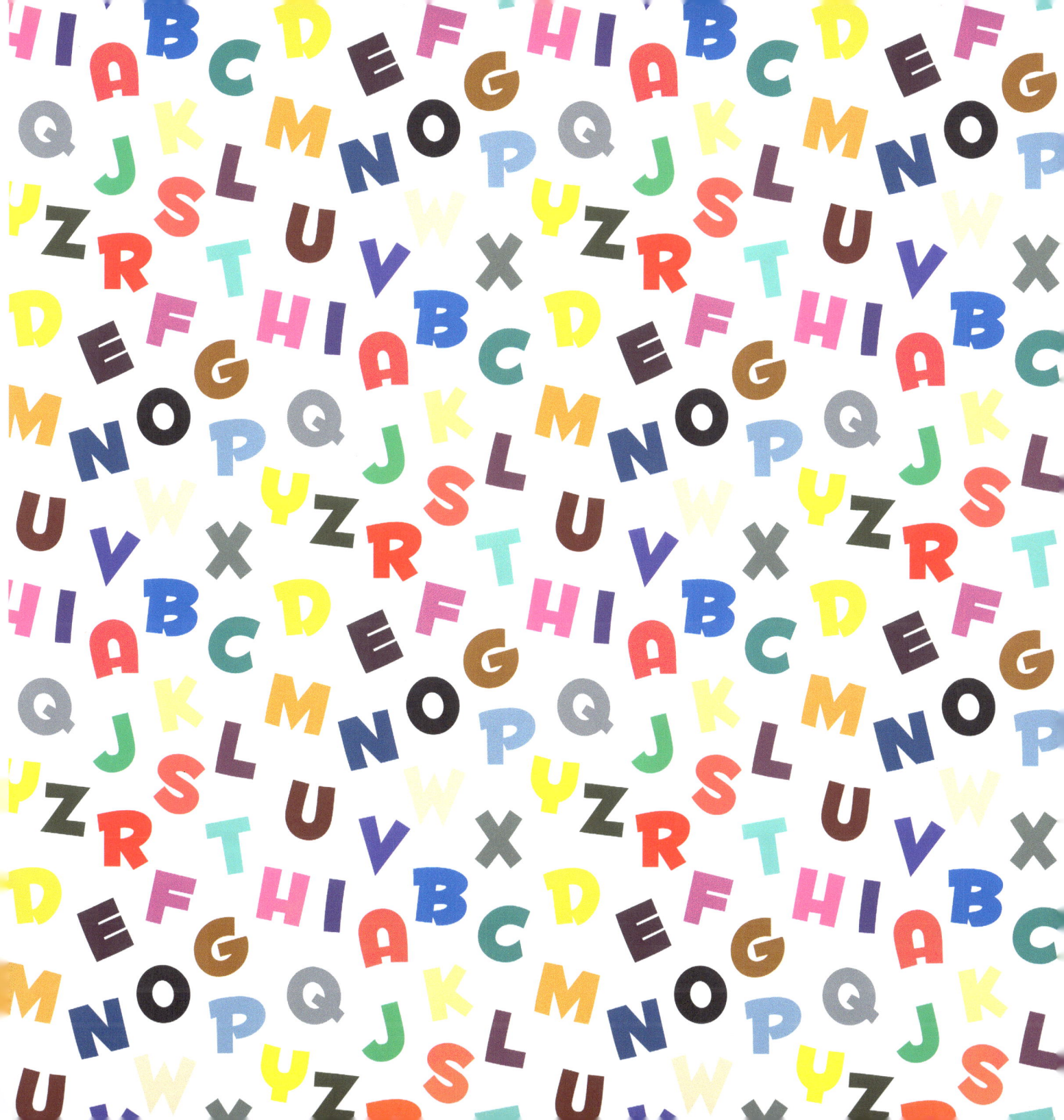

A

is for

alluring

amaranth

B

is for

beautiful

blue

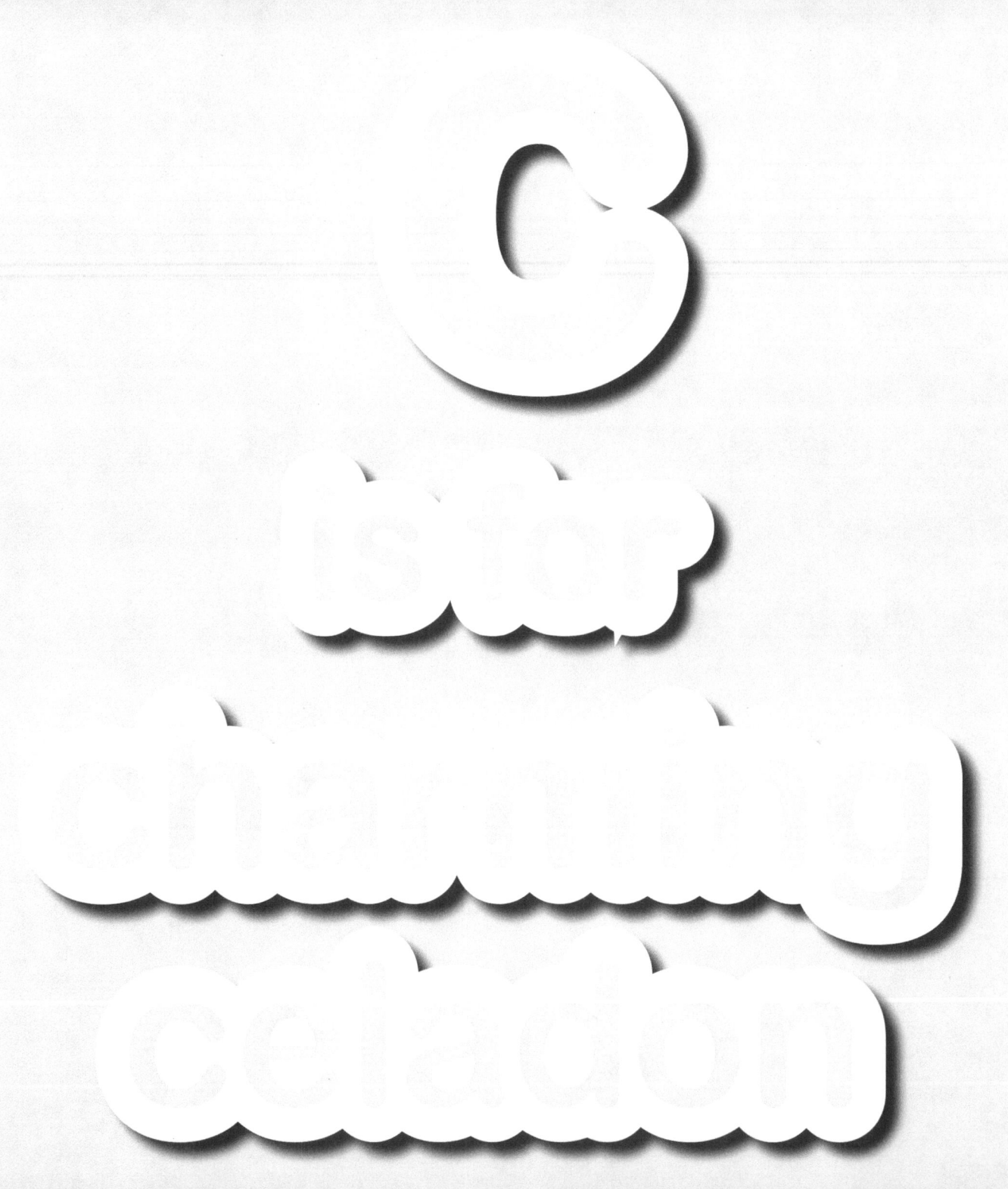

C
is for
charming
celadon

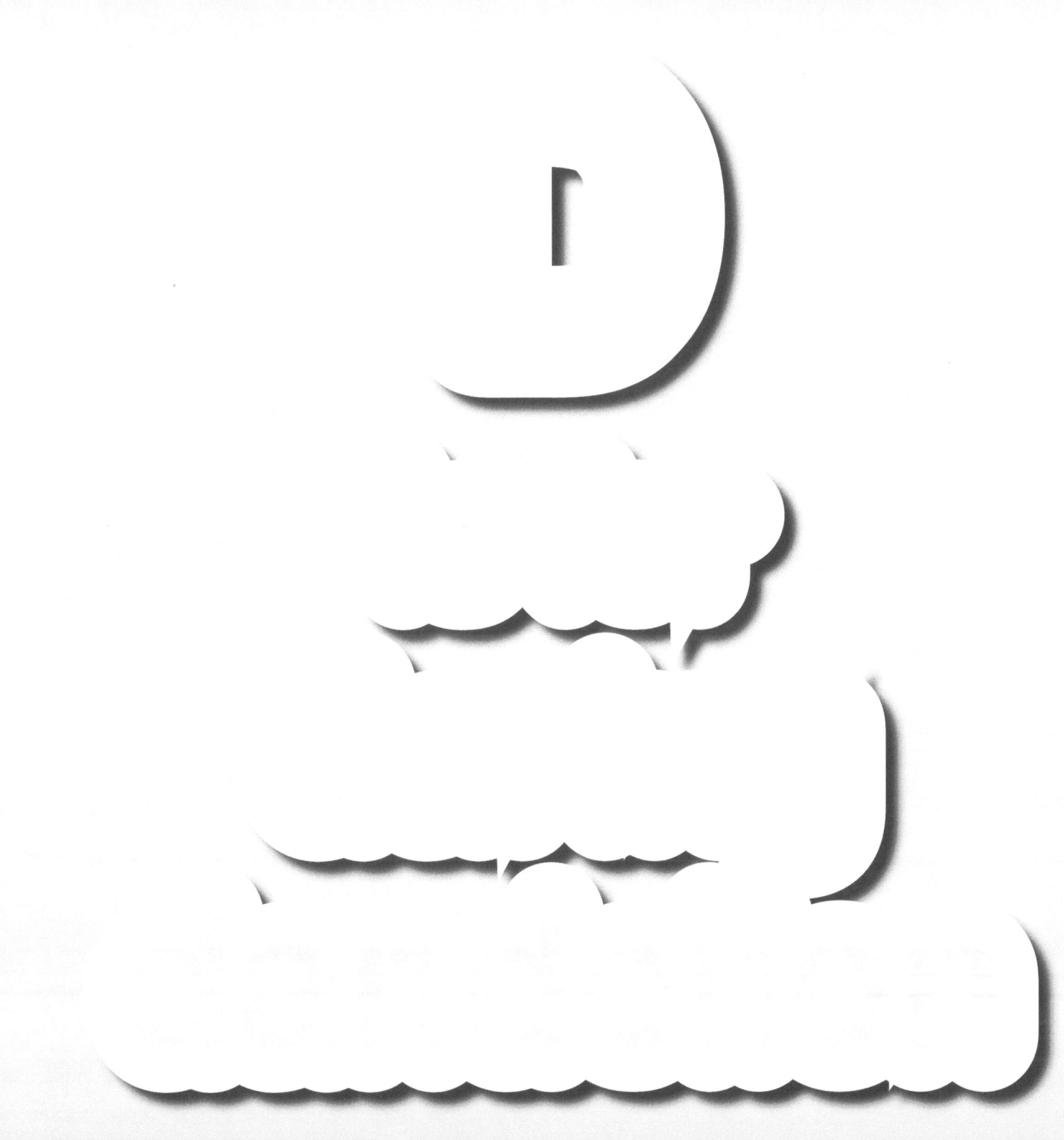

E

is for

excellent

eggplant

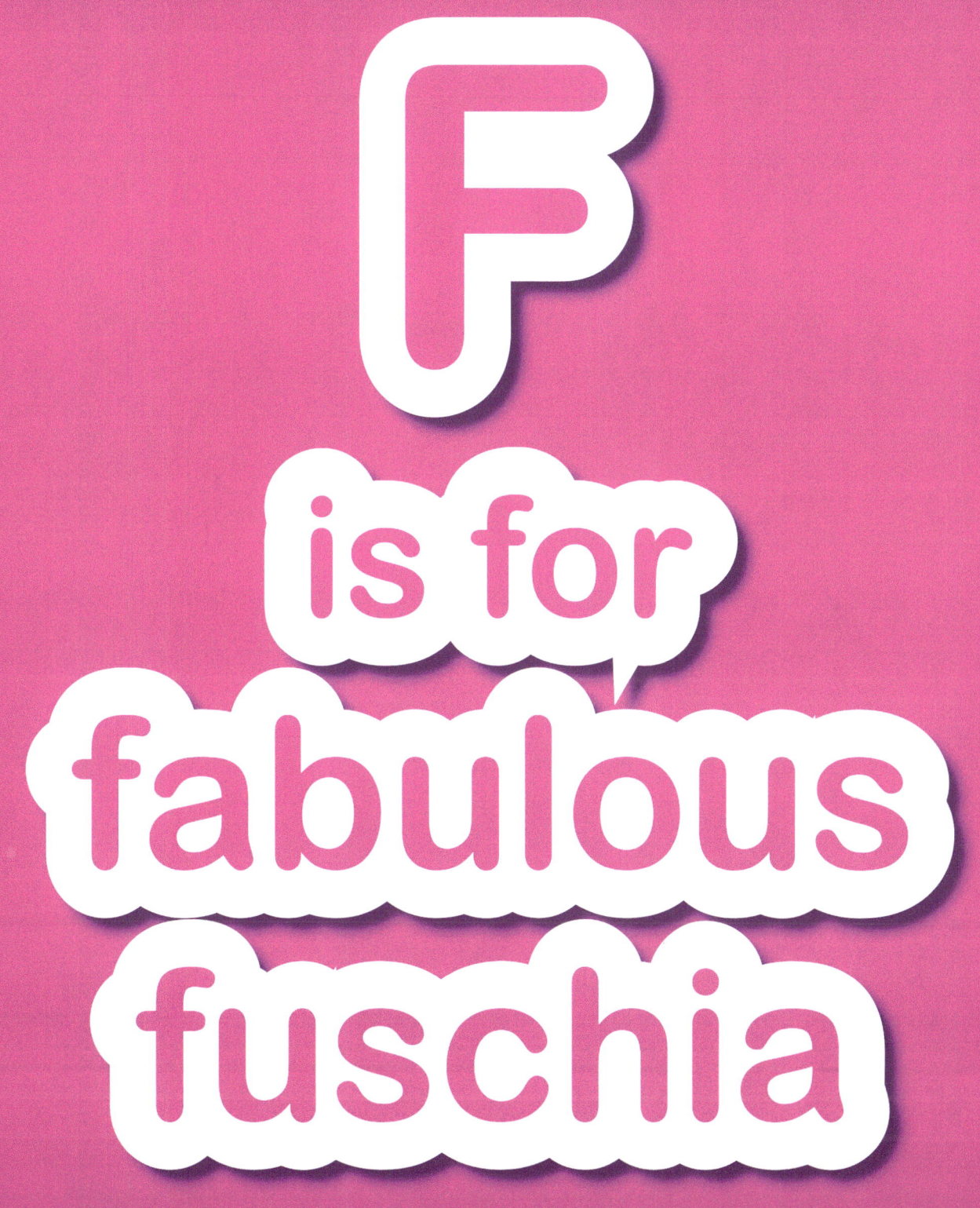

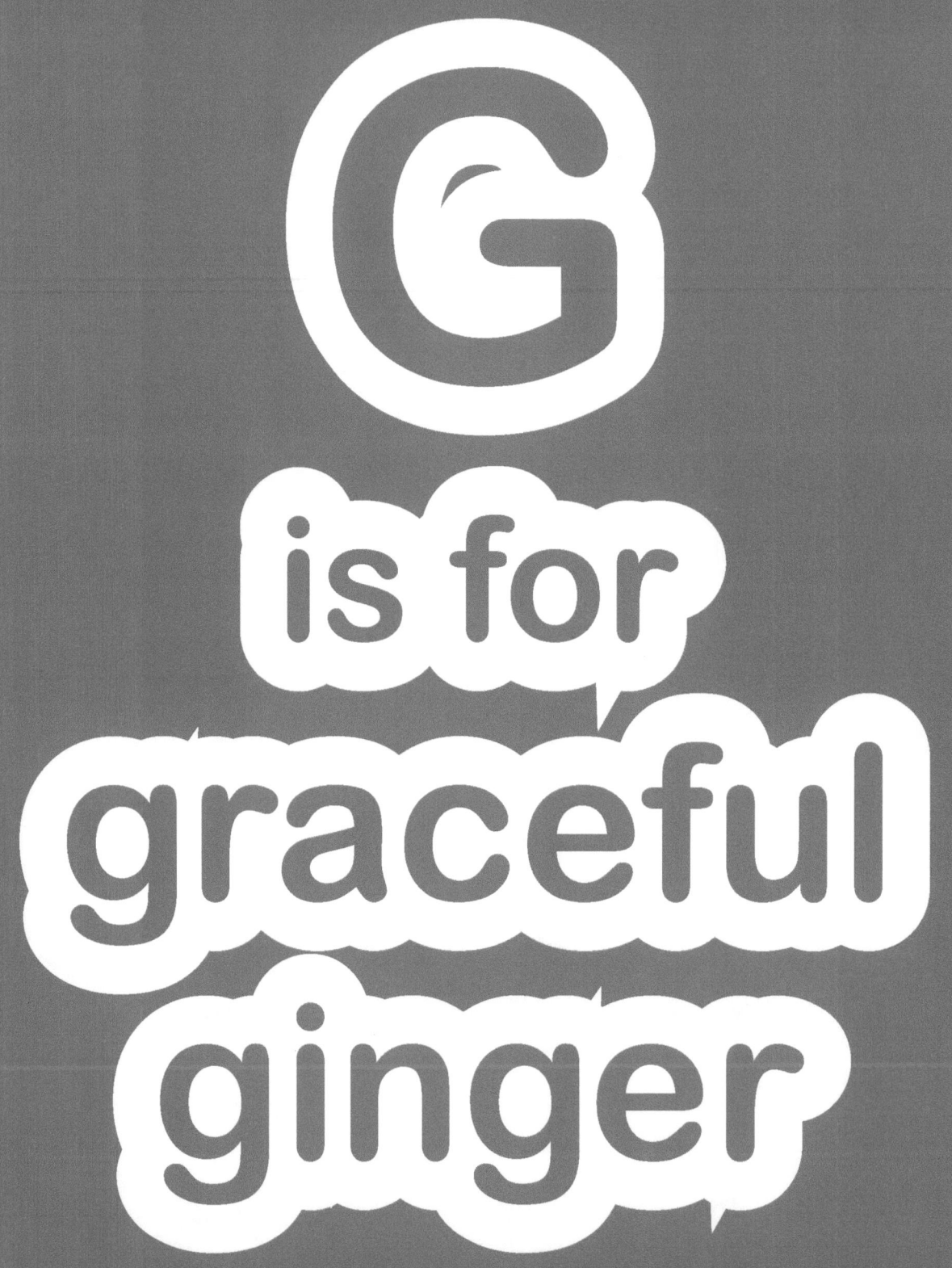

G

is for

graceful

ginger

H

is for

hip

hot pink

I

is for

irrestible

indigo

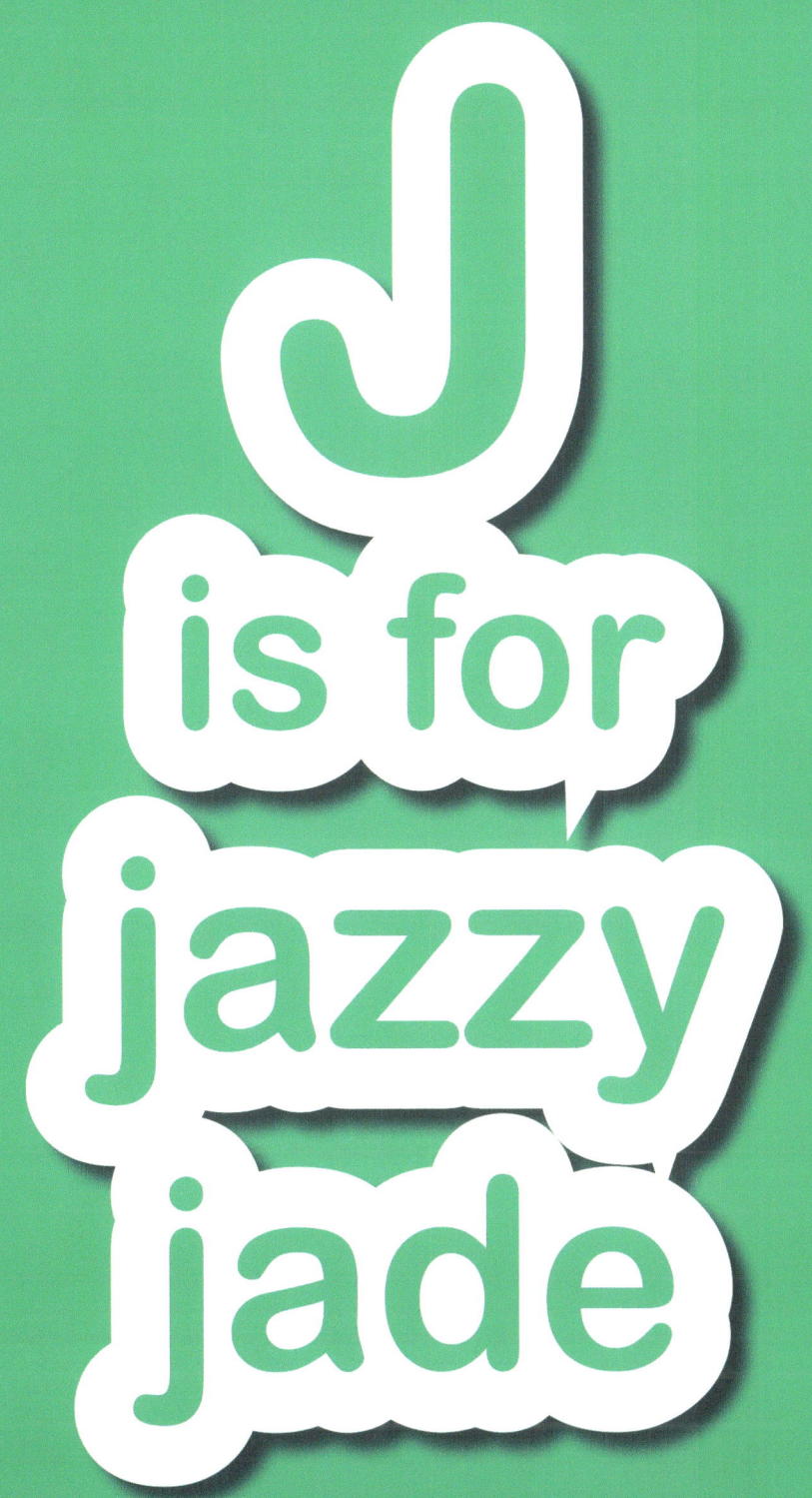

K

is for

kind

khaki

L

is for

lovely

lavender

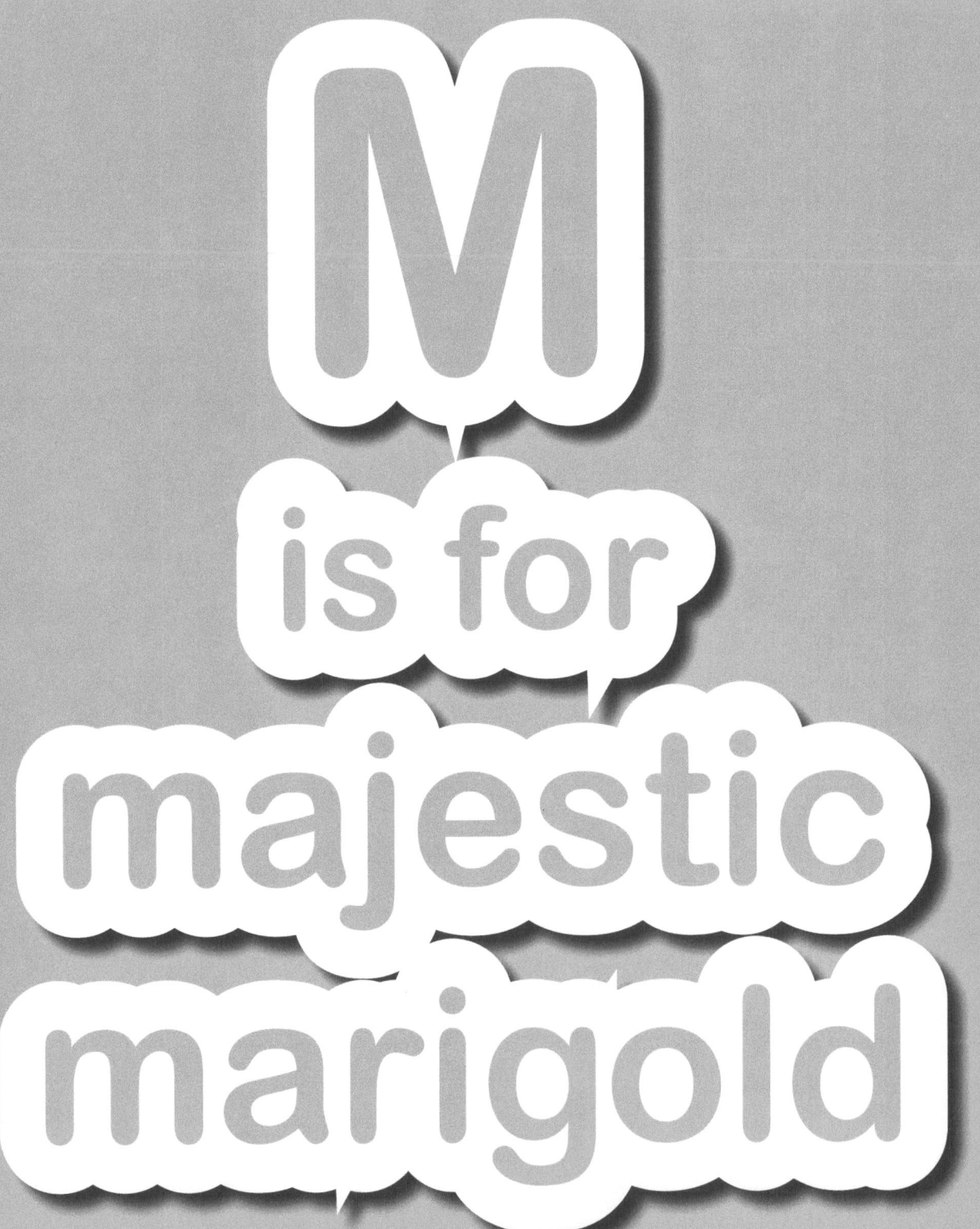

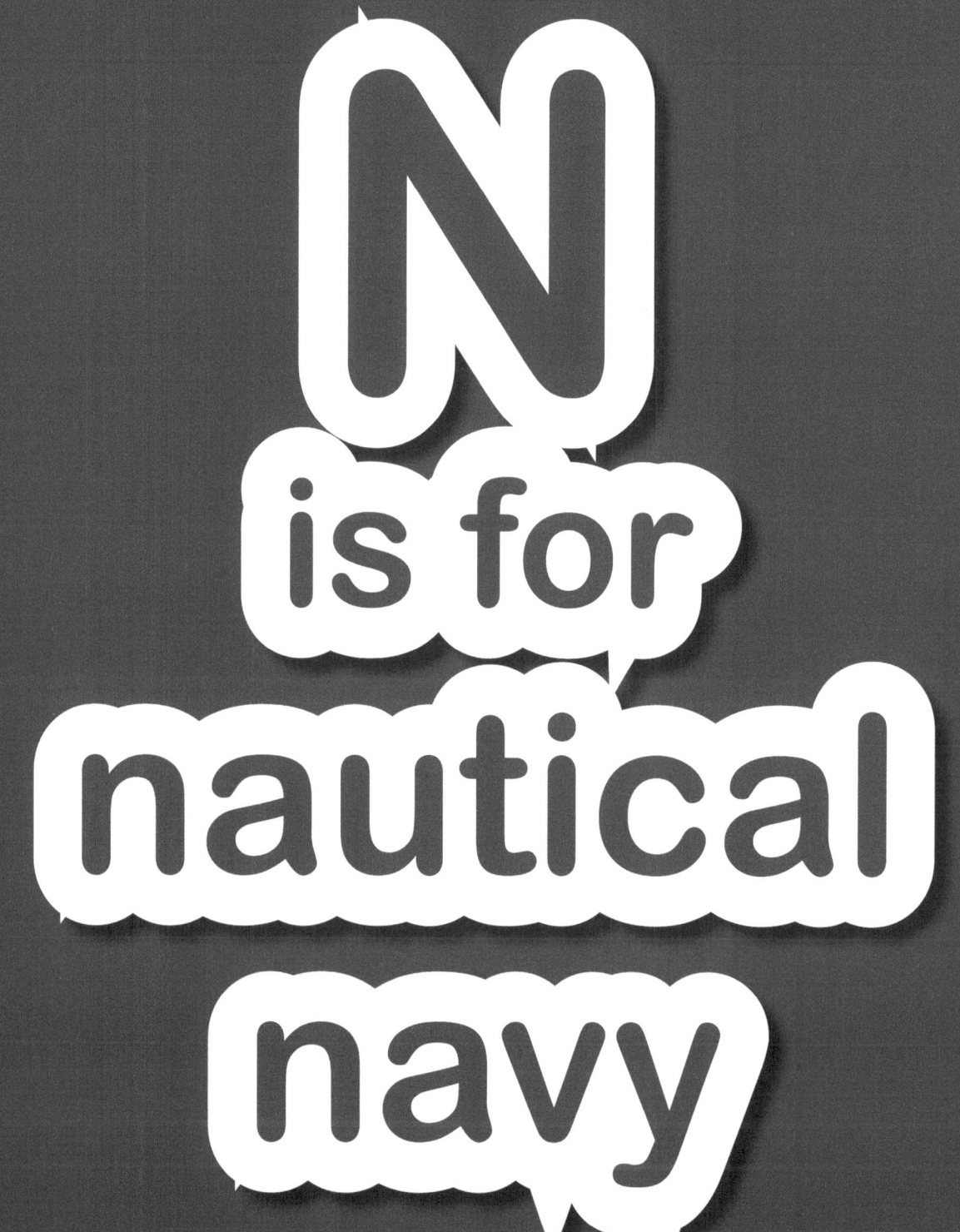

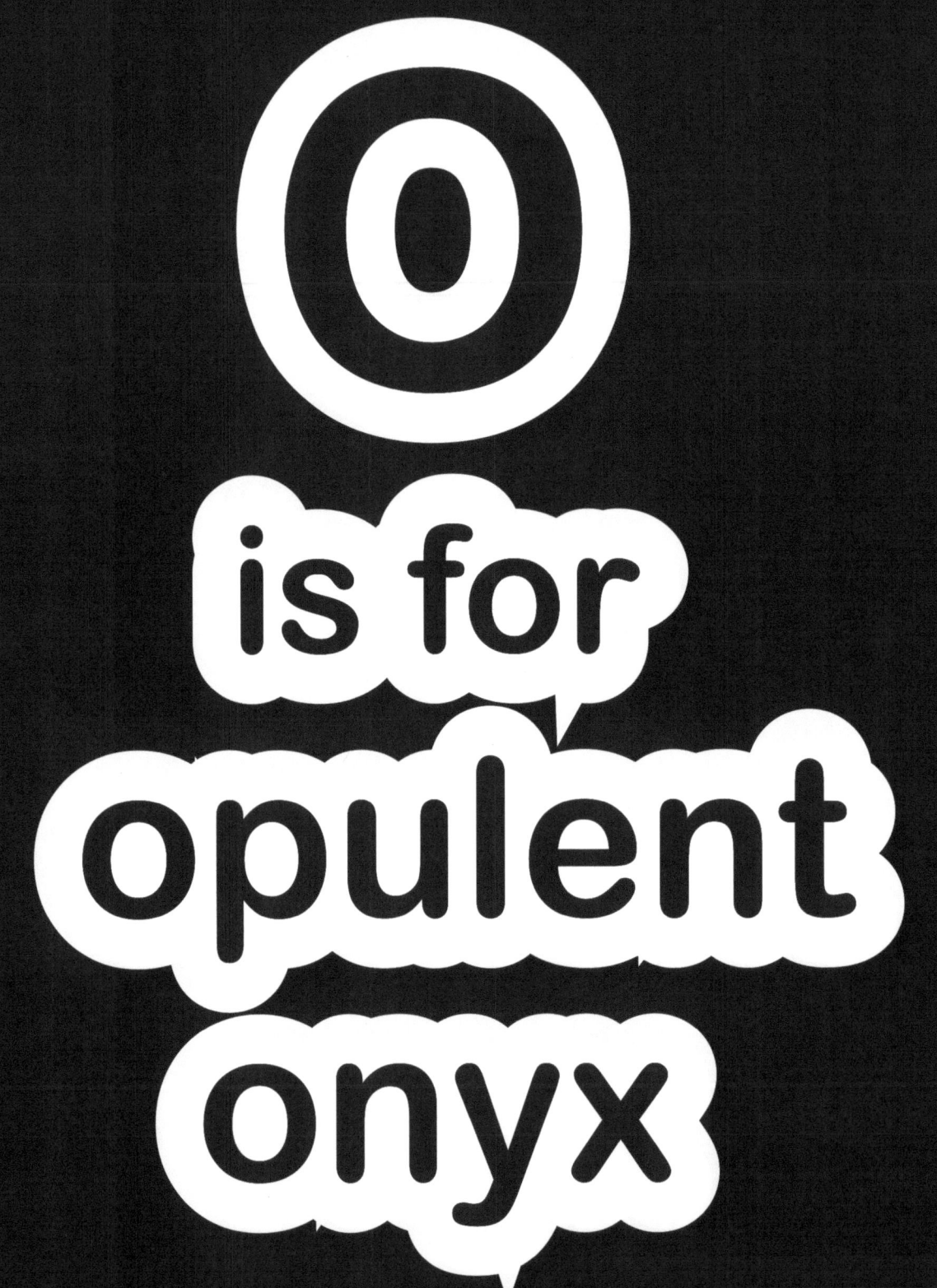

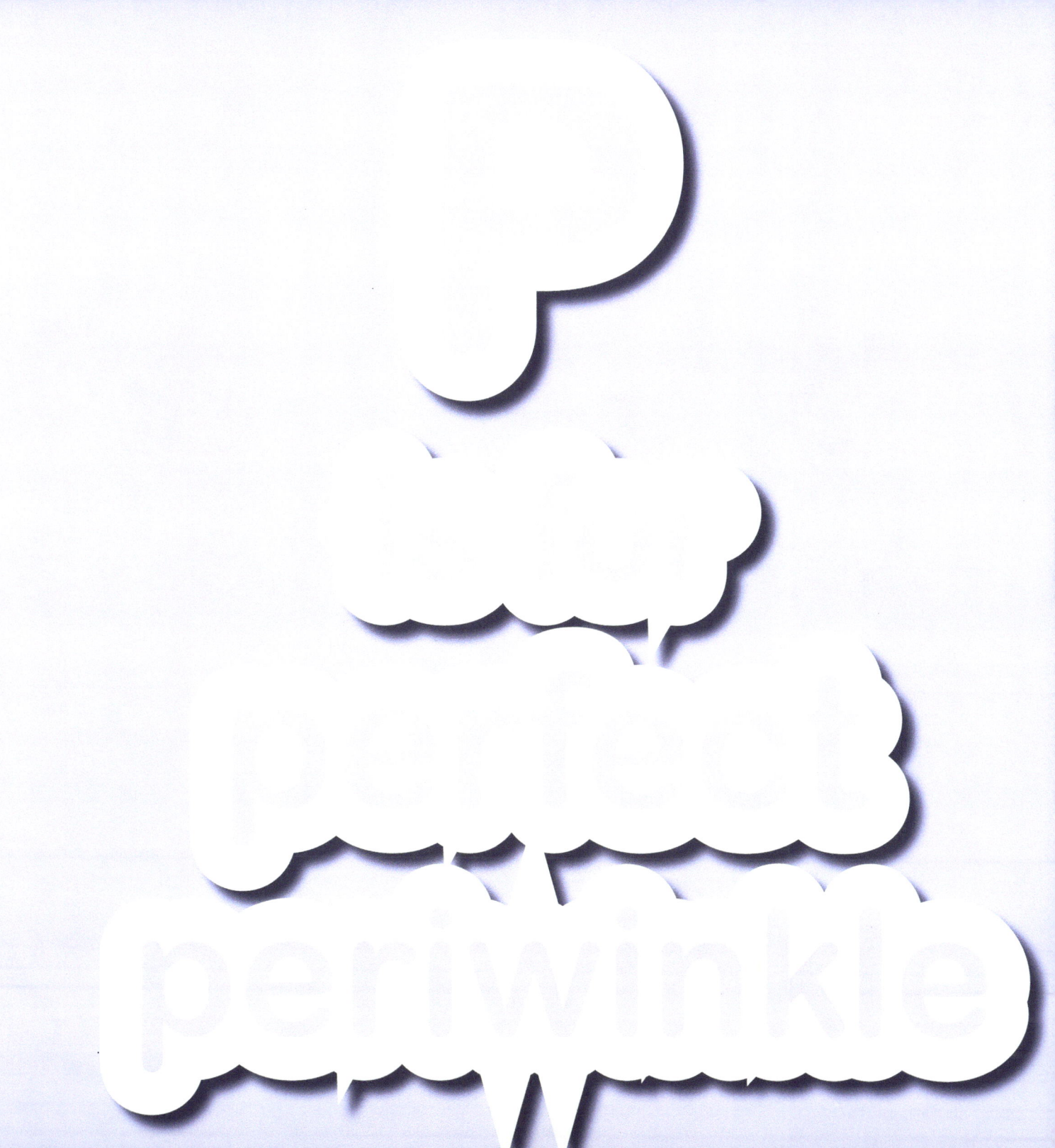

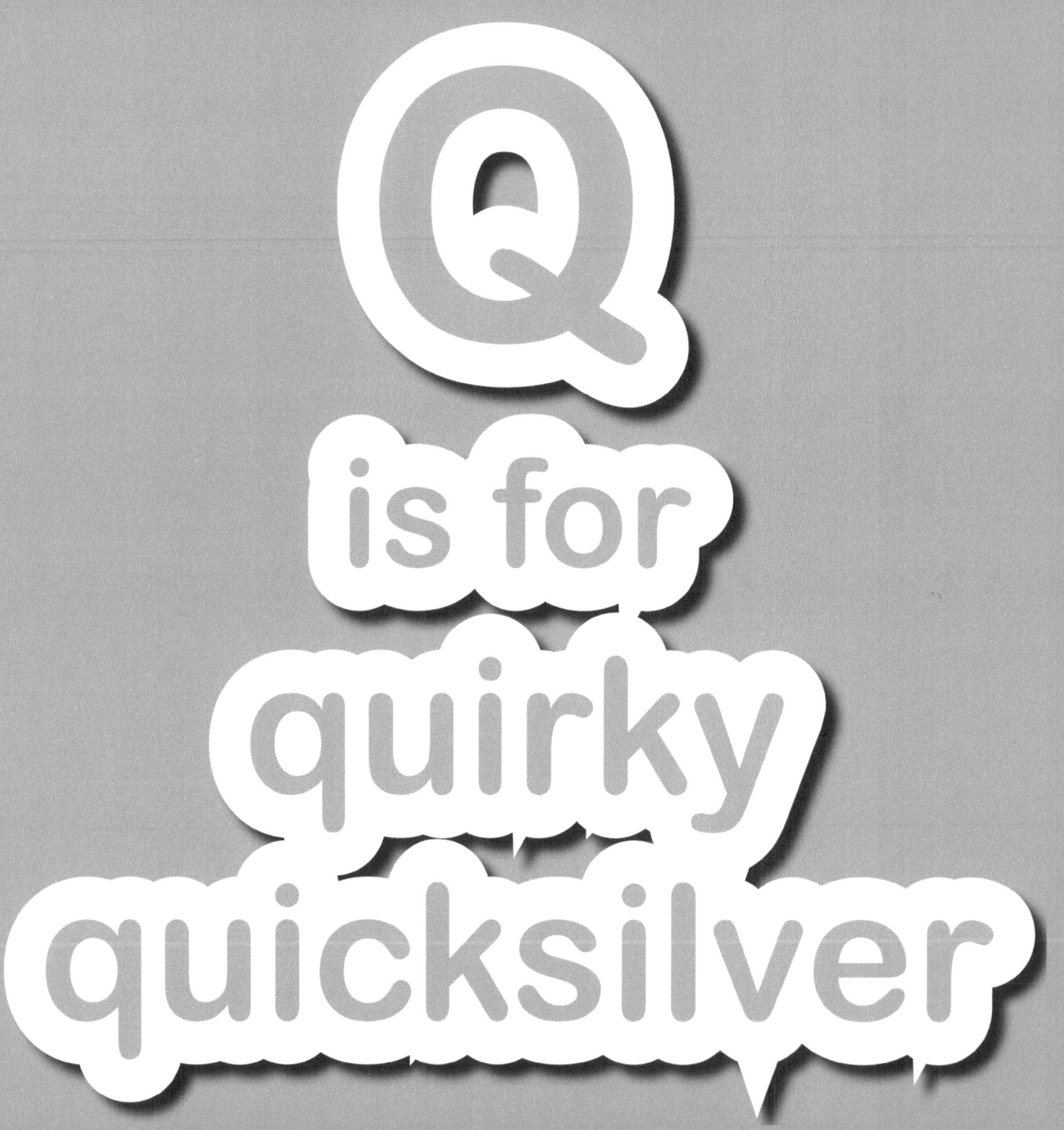

Q

is for

quirky

quicksilver

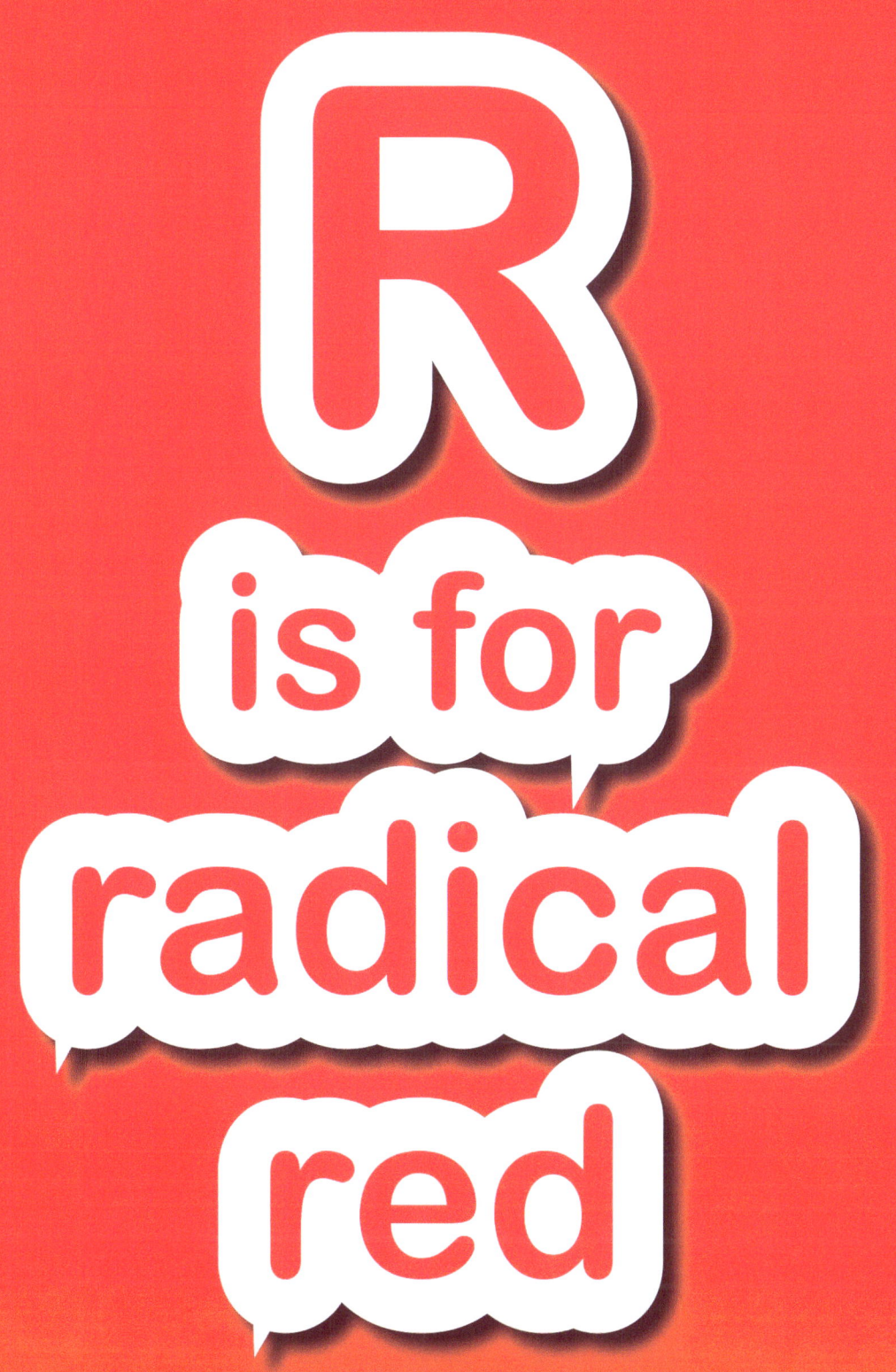

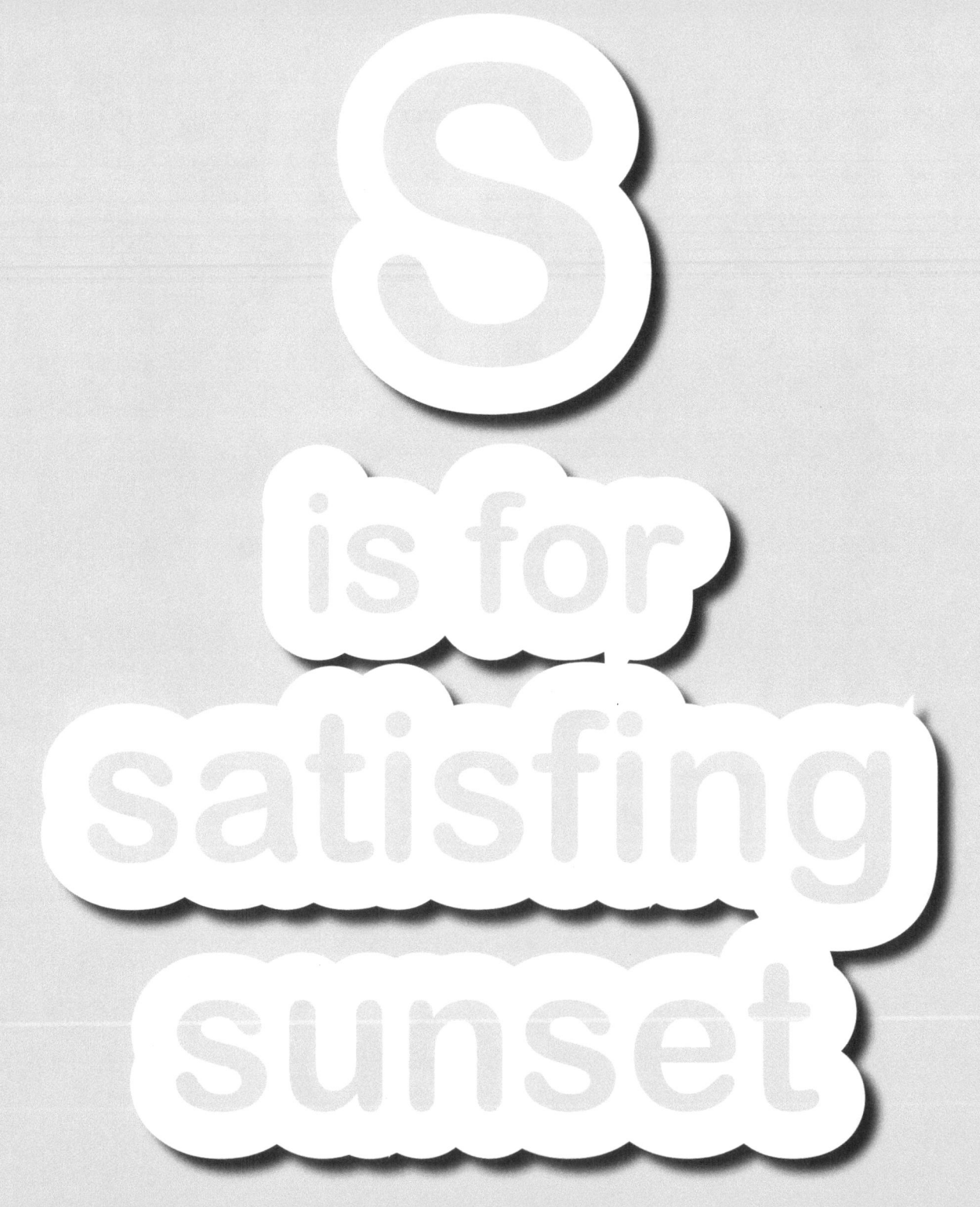

T

is for

tantalizing

turquoise

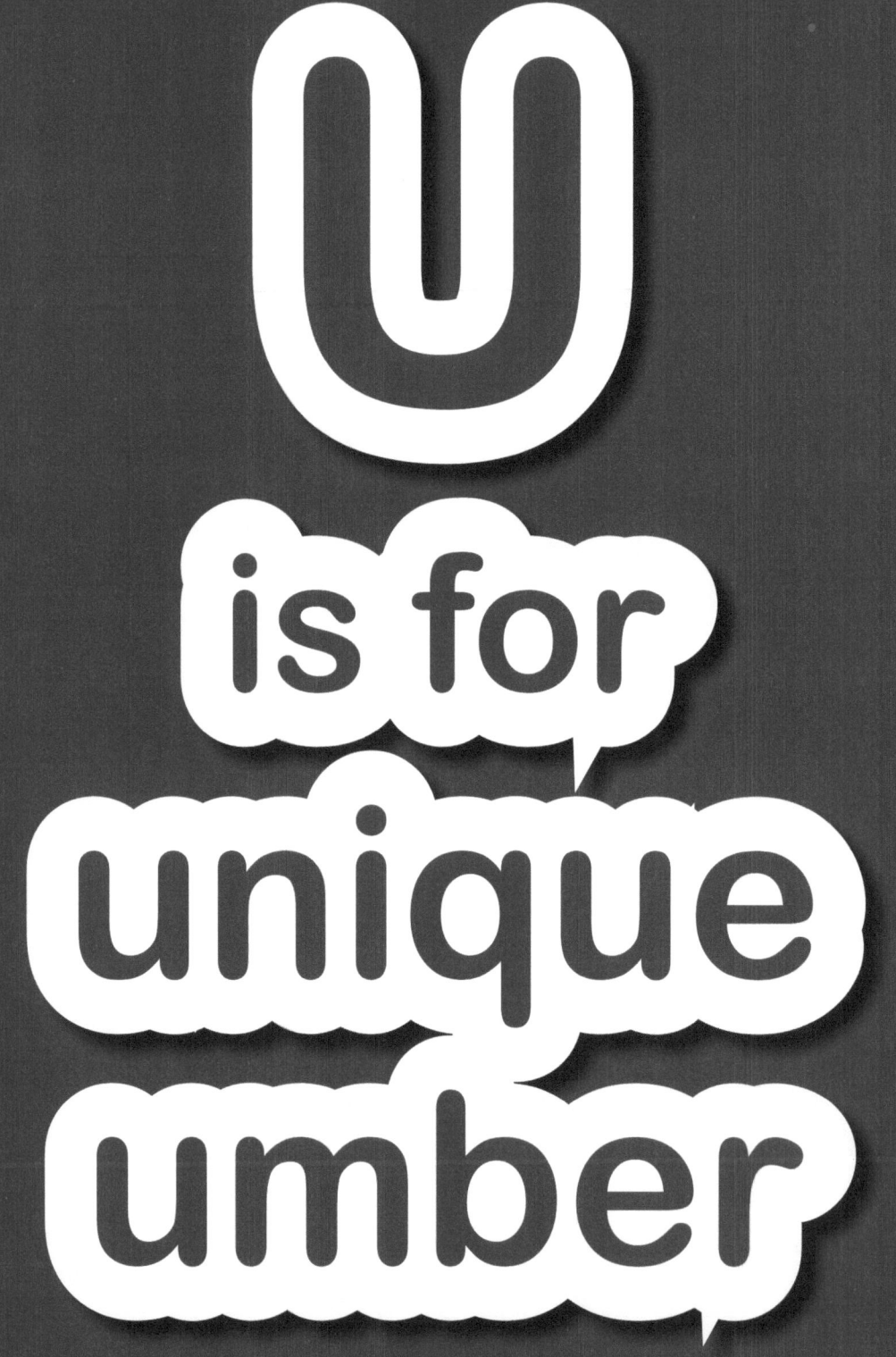

U

is for

unique
umber

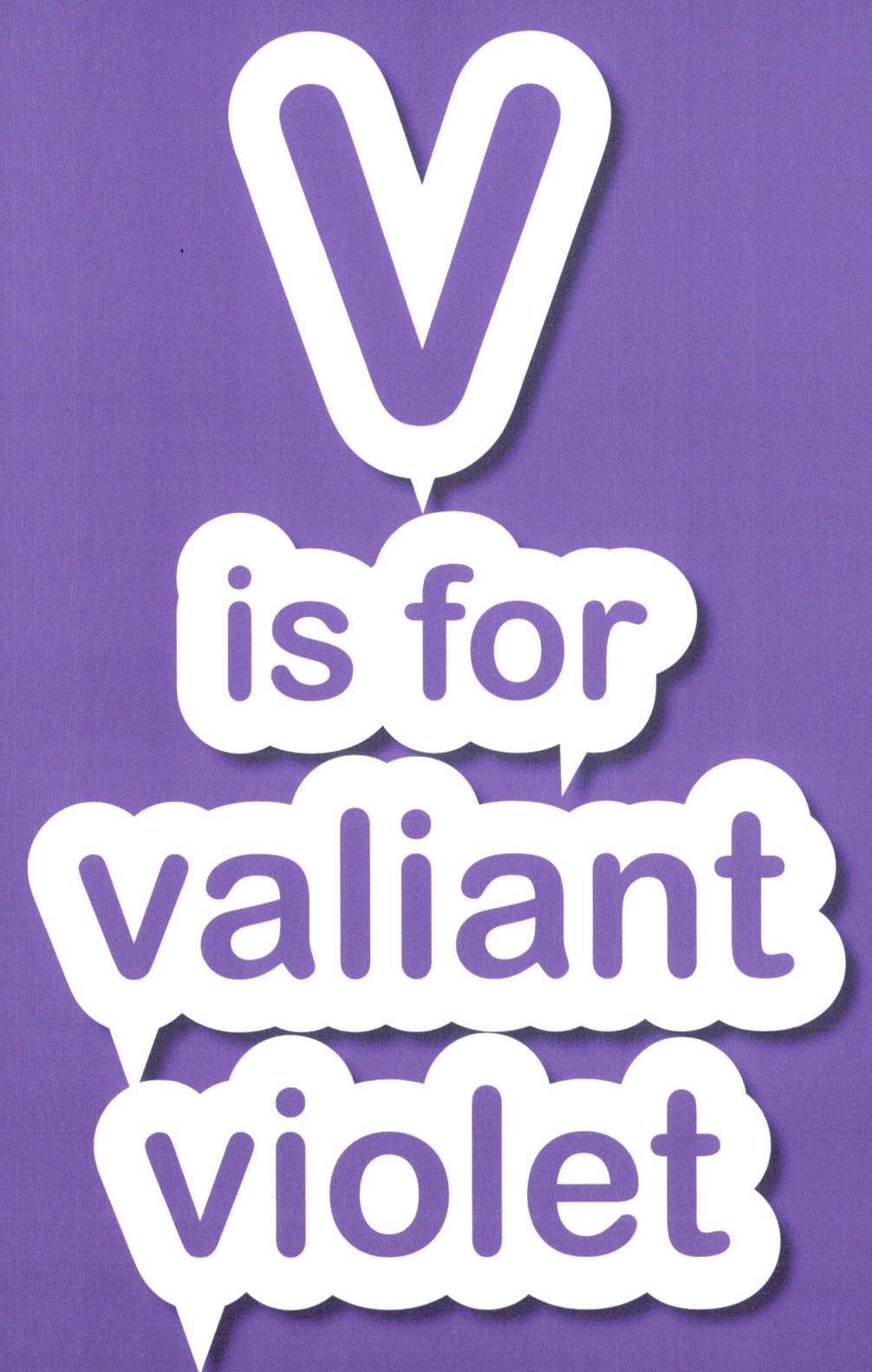

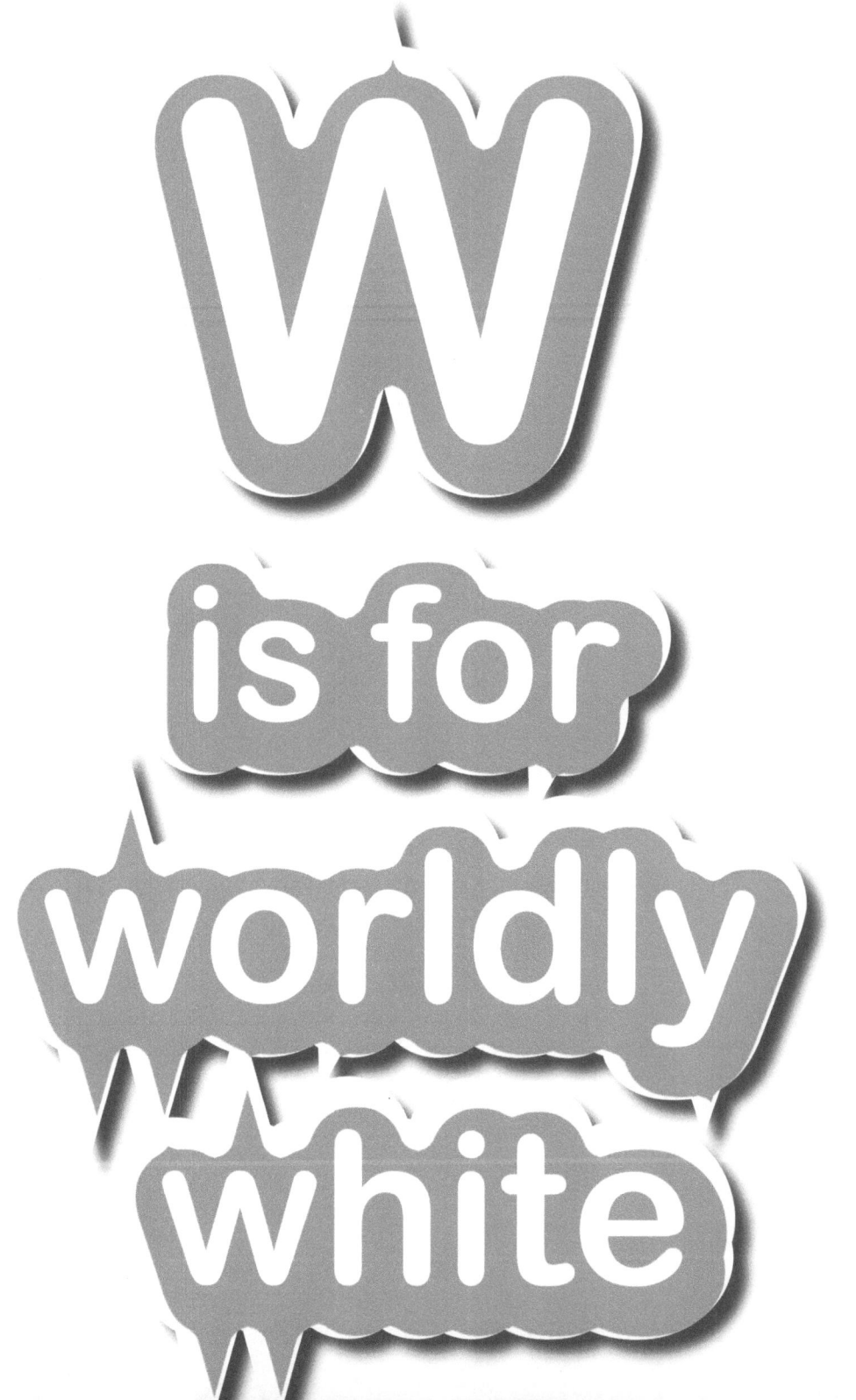

W

is for

worldly white

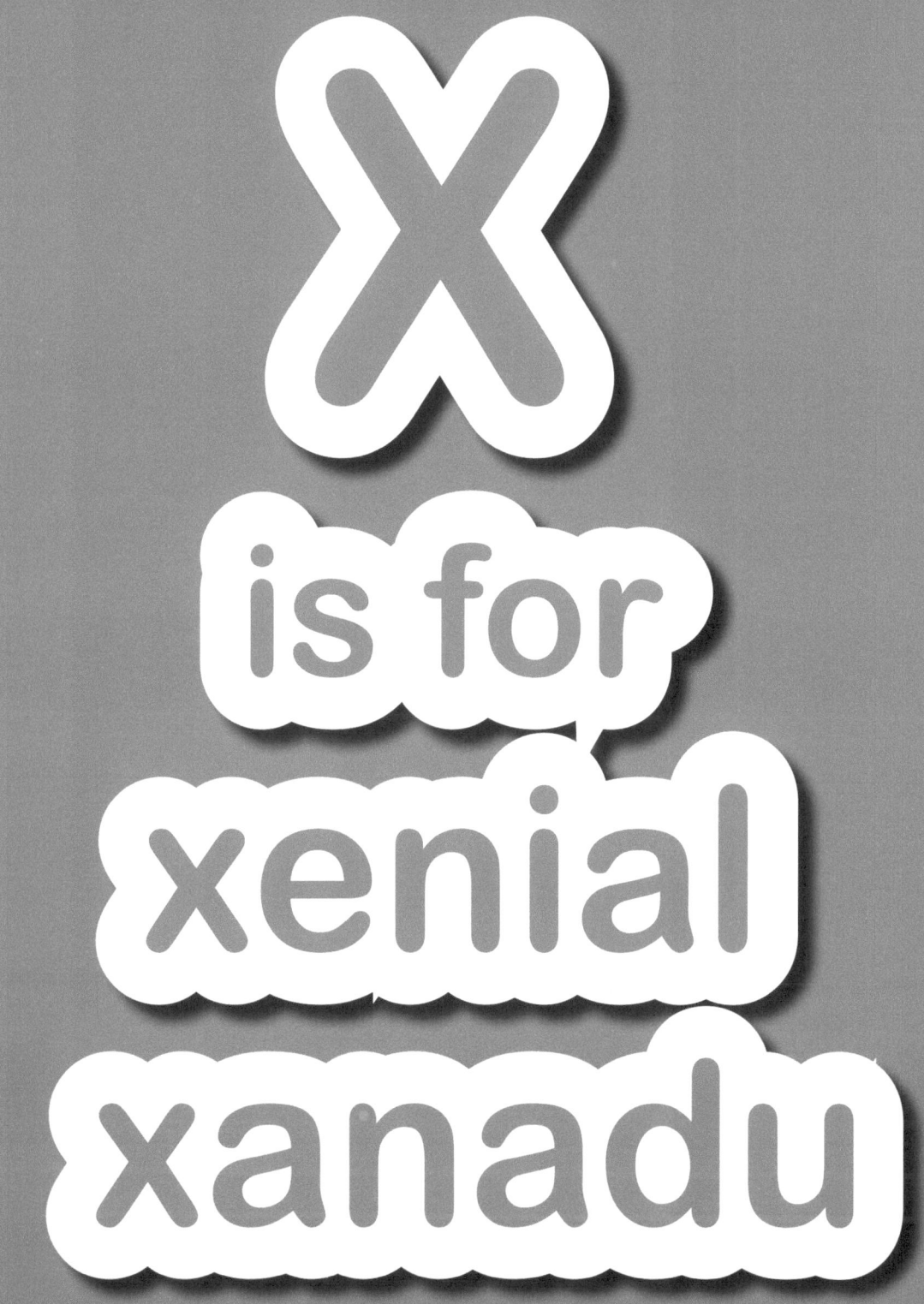

X

is for

xenial

xanadu

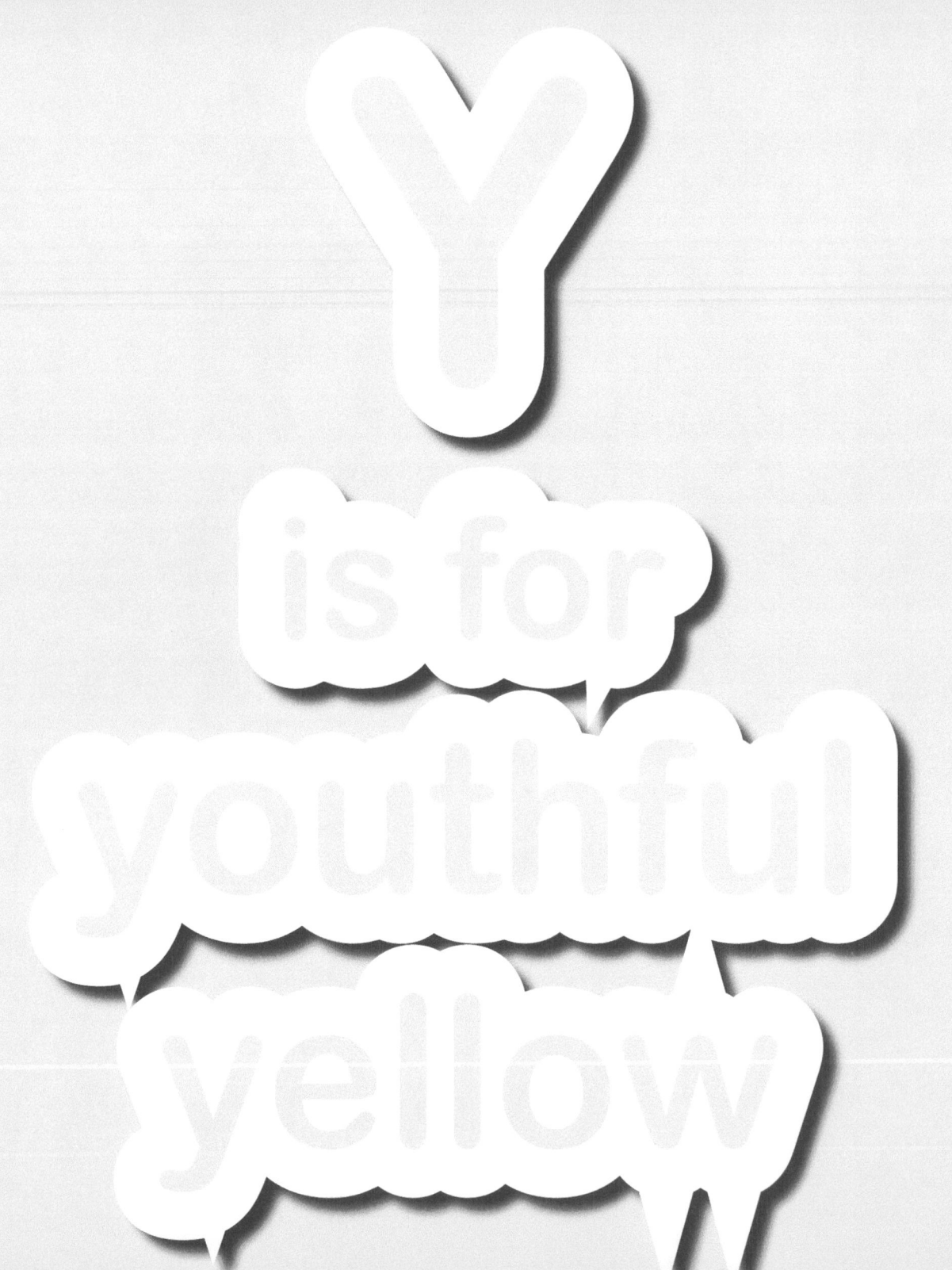

Z

is for

zestful

zucchini

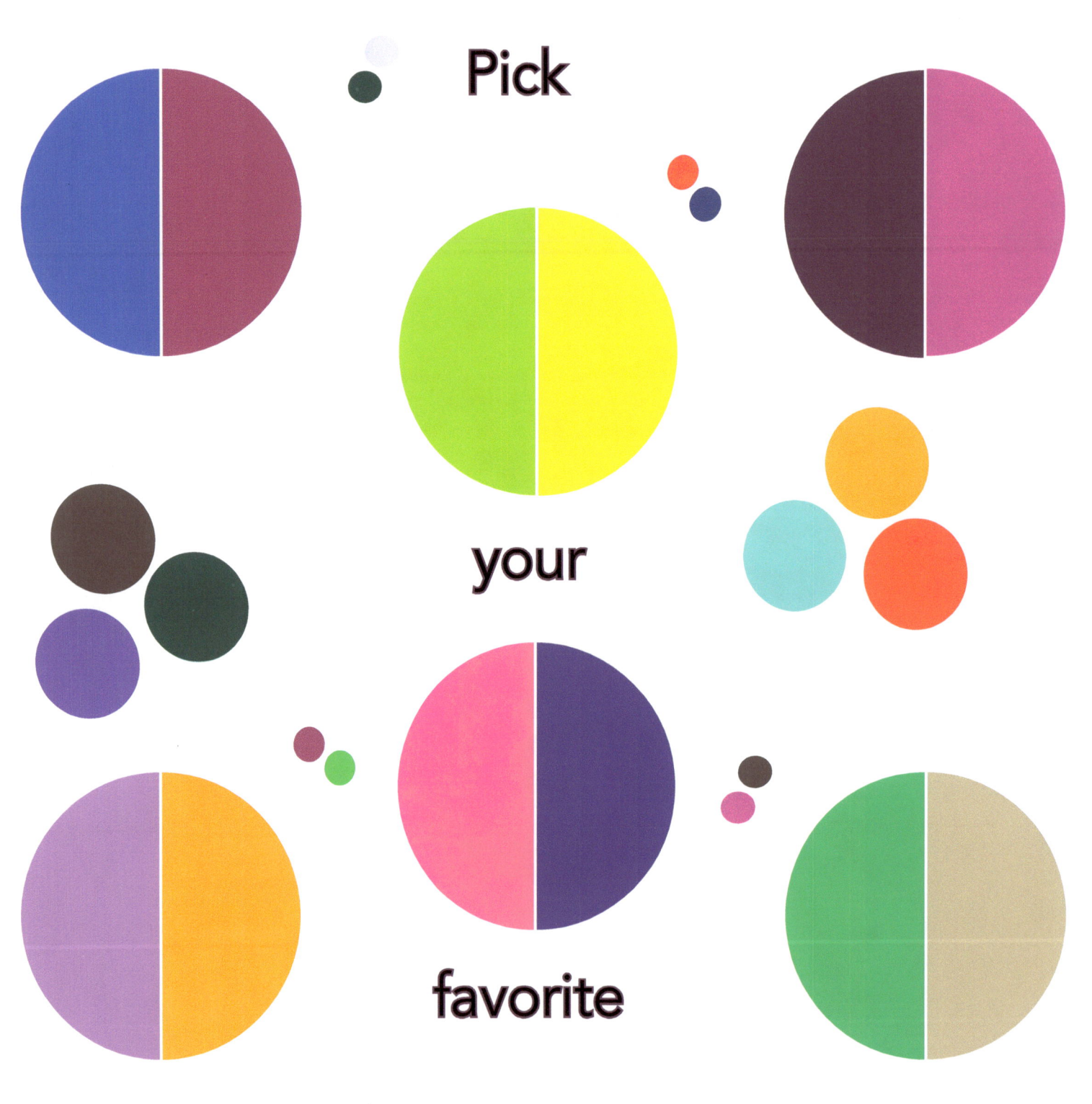

Pick your favorite

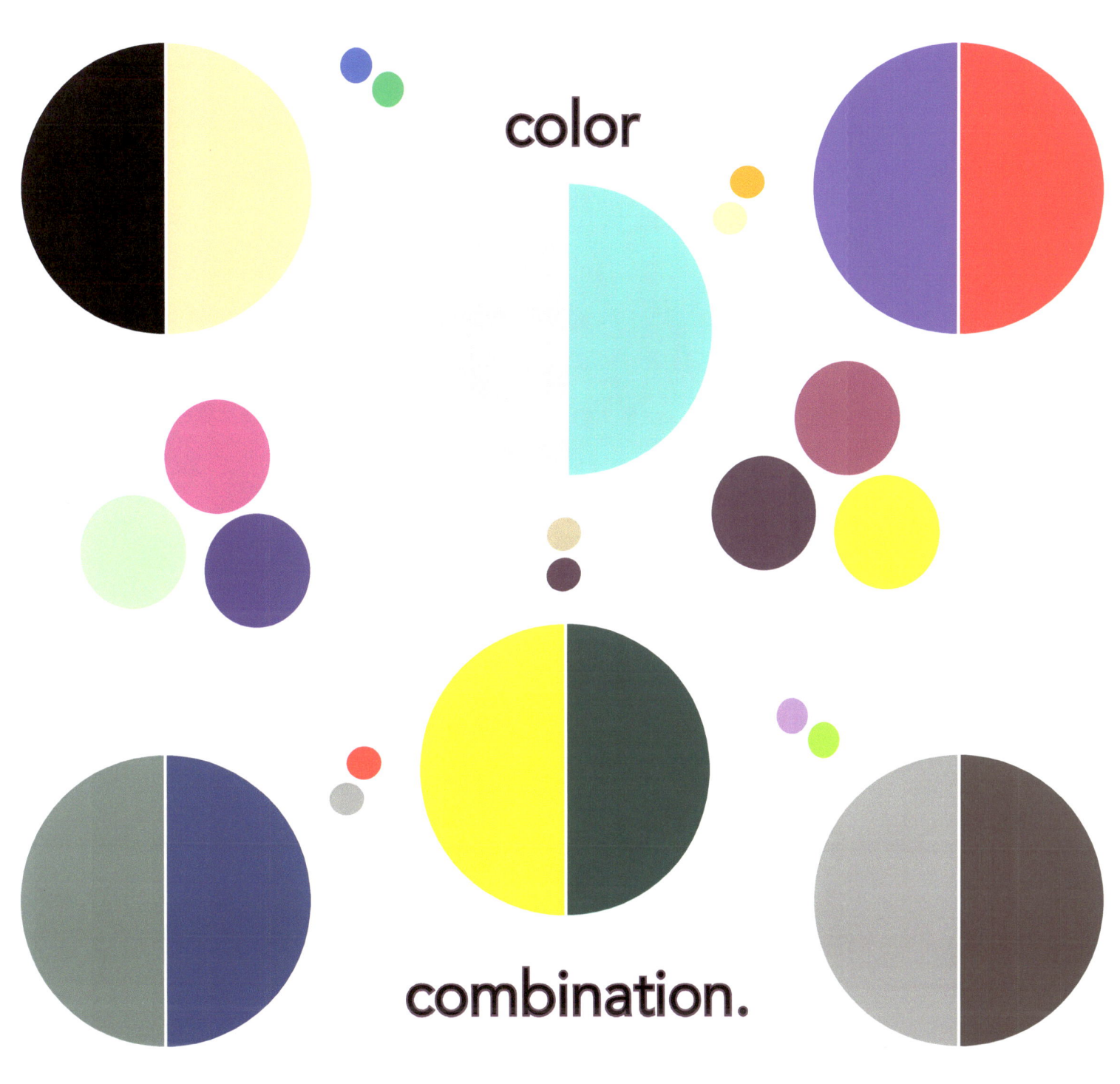

color

combination.

Can you sing the alphabet song?

A B C D

I J K L

Q R S T

Y Z

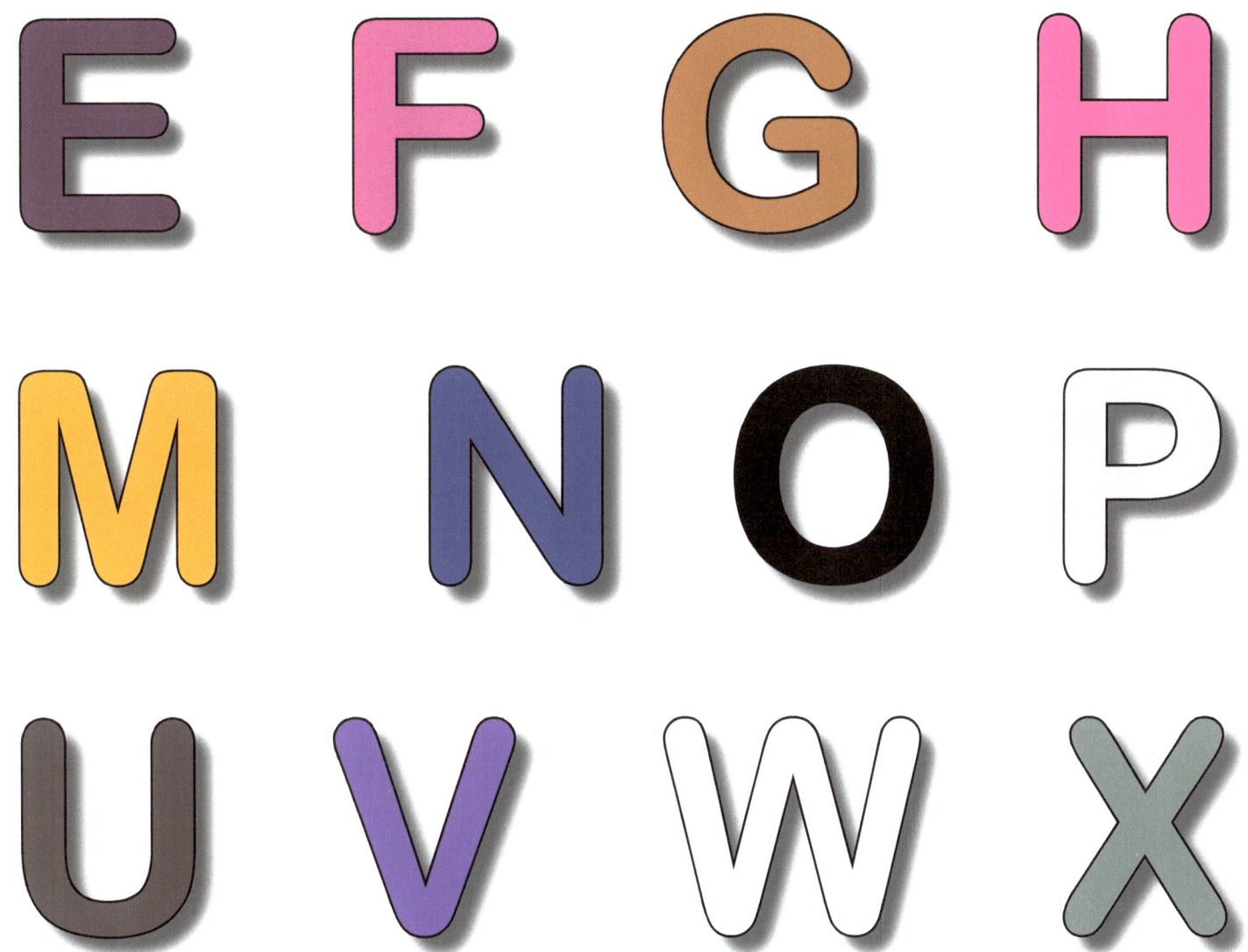

Pick your favorite color!

www.ingramcontent.com/pod-product-compliance
Lightning Source LLC
Chambersburg PA
CBHW050908180526
45159CB00007B/2830